Daily Mastery
Building Unshakable Foundations for Success

Table of Contents

The successful warrior is the average man, with laser-like focus.

— Bruce Lee

Chapter 1. Introduction

Imagine waking up every day fully equipped to conquer the world, overflowing with confidence to achieve all your goals. Welcome to our Special Report on "Daily Mastery: Building Unshakable Foundations for Success". This vibrant, engaging report isn't just a guide — think of it as the blueprint for creating your ideal life, one productive day at a time. Specially designed to empower, inspire, and propel you towards your dreams, we've packed this report with practical strategies, empowering narratives, scientifically-backed tactics, and transformative insights. If you've ever felt just within reach of success, or saw your dreams slip through your fingers, this is your chance to not only regain control but master your own destiny. So get ready to transform your everyday routines into strategic actions towards success. Let's start architecting your greatest accomplishment, shall we?

Chapter 2. Unlocking the Power of Positivity

Every winning strategy, each fulfilled dream, and all remarkable achievements have, at their core, positivity as their fundamental building block. The power of positivity is an inexhaustible fuel that propels us toward realizing our full potential, promoting not only self-improvement but also contributing to the overall well-being of those around us. It couples the daily sunset with an eagerness for the sunrise, transforming our perspective of the world, and honing in on opportunities rather than obstacles. The concept of positivity is not just an abstract idea; it is a veritable, tangible force that has the potential to change lives dramatically, and this chapter will delve deeply into its various facets.

2.1. The Science Behind Positivity

First, let us tackle the scientific perspective. Recent studies in the realm of psychology and neuroscience have found definitive links between a positive mindset and a variety of enhanced life outcomes, including better physical health, improved mental wellbeing, increased lifespan, and higher rates of success in personal and professional realms. For instance, the "broaden and build" theory proposed by psychologist Barbara Fredrickson proposes that positive emotions enlarge cognitive resources, thereby enabling a more creative, open-minded perspective and fostering the development of useful and enduring skills.

In another research, a study conducted on nuns explored the relationship between positivity and longevity. The nuns who expressed more positive emotions in their early life lived considerably longer than those who maintained a more negative or neutral perspective. Other experiments have found that optimism contributes to a stronger immune response, suggesting an inseparable link between body and mind.

2.2. Cultivating a Positive Mindset

Now that we have explored the science that backs up the benefits of positivity, let's delve into how you can foster a positive mindset in your everyday life. Understand that being positive doesn't mean ignoring the negatives. Rather, it's about choosing to see difficulties as opportunities for learning and growth. It's an acknowledge-and-adjust approach where we recognize the challenges that punctuate our journey through life but choose to focus on solutions rather than dwell on the problems.

One highly effective method of cultivating positivity is through the practice of gratitude. Scientific studies have expounded on the fact that those who actively practice gratitude have lower stress levels, improved mental alertness, physical wellness, and greater happiness. Begin by keeping a gratitude journal where you write down three things you are thankful for each day. This strengthens the neural pathways that trigger a positive emotional state, thereby rewiring your brain to look for the good in every situation.

2.3. Harnessing the Power of Positive Affirmations

Positive affirmations are another powerful tool in your positivity arsenal. These are statements that you repeat to yourself to build a positive internal dialogue. They can combat negative thought patterns, inspire change, and reinforce positive beliefs or behaviors. Do not simply state positive affirmations; embrace and embody them, feeling the emotions associated with their meanings. This will help reinforce the neural pathways responsible for these affirmation-induced positive mental health outcomes.

2.4. Embracing Positivity Through Healthy Relationships

Our interactions and relationships play a significant role in shaping our mindset. Therefore, surrounding yourself with positive influences is crucial. This doesn't just imply avoiding negative people; it refers to cultivating relationships with individuals who uplift and challenge you, who inspire growth and contest complacency. In cultivating these relationships, one can consistently maintain positivity and resilience in the face of adversity.

2.5. Positivity: A Power, Not a Pandora's Box

A caveat in our positivity exploration: it is important to not mistake blind optimism for positivity. Being positive does not mean turning a blind eye to issues that need your attention or not acknowledging feelings of sadness or anger. It means choosing to focus on the most beneficial aspects of a situation and finding potential solutions instead of sprawling in the problem. Positivity, when reigned wisely, becomes a powerful steering wheel directing the course of our life.

Integrating these strategies into your everyday life can lead to empowering transformations that extend beyond the realm of personal development. By unlocking the power of positivity, you're not only setting yourself up for success but also raising the bar for what can be universally achieved. This potent weapon, harnessed correctly, can truly make you the master of your destiny. Stay tuned as we continue to explore more building blocks for your path to daily mastery.

Chapter 3. Mastering Your Morning Rituals: The Blueprint

Just as the iconic pyramid is built from its base, an individual's success is rooted in the establishment of well-formed daily habits. At the forefront of these habits, we find the morning ritual: rituals that not only stir the body into action but also prime the mind for the cascades of challenges and opportunities the day is bound to bring. Mastering one's morning rituals involves implementing a strategy. A blueprint, precisely, which guides us away from morning disarray and sets the stage for a day of accomplishment and fulfillment. The steps and concepts outlined in this chapter serve as a manual towards crafting an effective morning routine, aimed at promoting productivity and boosting overall well-being.

3.1. Setting the Stage for A Productive Morning

It all starts with laying a conducive foundation for your mornings. It's about placing strategic thought into preparing for the next day. To ensure you are waking up in a serene environment, declutter and organize your bedroom the night before. You may also want to buy an alarm clock to avoid screen time first thing in the morning. Most importantly, you must set a consistent wake-up time, signaling the brain to gear up for a routine, which, over time, becomes far easier to follow.

3.2. Waking Up with Purpose

When the alarm goes off, instead of succumbing to the allure of the snooze button, leap out of bed with purpose. Understand that each morning presents a fresh chance to make progress towards your goals. Cultivate a sense of gratitude as you take your first breaths of the day, setting the tone for positivity and abundance that can reverberate throughout your hours.

3.3. Hydrating and Nourishing the Body

After hours of sleep, our bodies are in a slightly dehydrated state. Starting the day with a glass of water replenishes essential fluids, activating our body's functions. You could even add a dash of lemon for an extra jolt of Vitamin C. Additionally, breakfast, as the literal break from our overnight fast, fuels us with the energy we need, both mentally and physically, to meet the day's demands. Invest in a balanced breakfast, one that blends proteins, fiber, and healthy fats to provide a steady energy release throughout the morning. Examples might include oatmeal topped with a handful of nuts and berries, or an egg-white omelet filled with an assortment of colorful veggies.

3.4. Physical Vitality: The Power of Movement

Engaging in some form of exercise in the morning can be transformative. Regular morning exercise kickstarts your metabolism, enhances focus, and lifts your mood. Whether it's a brisk walk around the block, a yoga flow, or even a full-blown workout session, the key is consistency.

3.5. Nourishing the Mind: Mental Fitness

Just as our bodies need nourishment and exercise, our minds require attention and conditioning for optimal performance. Here, strategies such as meditation, mindfulness exercises, or journaling can be highly effective. These practices anchor us to the present moment, clear mental clutter, and promote better emotional regulation, helping us face the daily grind with an unshakeable state of tranquility.

3.6. Goal Setting and Prioritization: A Directed Day

Now that you've addressed both physical and psychological dimensions, it's time to steer the day in the direction you desire. This is effectively done through goal setting and prioritization. Set goals for the day that align with your long-term objectives, then prioritize these tasks in order of their importance and urgency. Having a clear roadmap provides a sense of direction, boosts your focus, and promotes productivity.

Mastering your mornings, indeed, is not a destiny reached overnight. It involves careful contemplation, deliberate crafting, and, most importantly, relentless execution. However, once honed, these rituals act as your personal blueprint, establishing the bedrock for a day of success and a life of accomplishment. It's time to rise above the mediocrity of haphazard beginnings and embrace the mastery of deliberate mornings.

Chapter 4. Fueling Up: Nutritional Strategies for Supercharged Productivity

Without a doubt, nutrition forms the keystone of our overall health and well-being, deftly underpinning every aspect of our lives. It is the gasoline that drives the complicated machinery of the human body, and plays a critical role in our levels of productivity and focus. This chapter delves deep into the relationship between nutrition and productivity, offering compelling, insightful strategies for an optimally fuelled life.

4.1. The Fuel-Productivity Connection

Before we delve into the nitty-gritty, it's important to understand the link between nutrition and productivity. Imagine starting your car in the morning but forgetting to fill up the gas. It gives you a few miles, but eventually, it sputters to a halt. This is a simple analogy but reflects our bodies accurately. Without adequate fuel, our bodies struggle to perform, our focus dwindles, and power needed to sustain productivity trickles to a near stop. That's why the right nutrition—the right 'fuel'—is integral to your productivity and overall well-being.

4.2. The Power of Protein

Protein forms the backbone of this strategy. A building block of every cell in your body, protein has been known to increase the production of neurotransmitters like dopamine and norepinephrine, both of which are crucial for maintaining focus and energy levels.

Incorporating lean protein sources like fish, turkey, eggs, Greek yogurt, and plant proteins into your meals can provide a steady stream of energy, keeping you fueled for a long productive day.

4.3. The Role of Hydration

Hydration is as necessary for the body as the fuel you put in your car. Even mild dehydration has been linked to decreased cognitive performance—namely focus, attention, and short-term memory. Keeping yourself hydrated with water, herbal teas, and natural juices boosts your metabolism, keeps your cognitive functions sharp, and keeps fatigue at bay.

4.4. Complex Carbohydrates: Sustainable Energy

Unlike simple sugars that cause a spike and subsequent crash in blood sugar levels, complex carbohydrates provide a steady, slow-release source of energy. Foods like whole grains, brown rice, oats, and fruits contain these carbohydrates that help maintain stable blood sugar levels, preventing energy crashes and promoting consistent focus and productivity.

4.5. The Impact of Fats: Good vs. Bad

Not all fats are created equal. Good fats, such as monounsaturated and polyunsaturated fats found in avocados, fatty fish, nuts, and olives, are incredibly beneficial for brain health. They improve cognition, memory, and facilitate neurotransmitter function, thereby supporting productivity. On the contrary, trans fats and saturated fats can hamper mental agility and should be limited.

4.6. Power of Micronutrients

Vitamins and minerals may not provide energy, but they are essential in the energy production process. Iron, B-vitamins, and magnesium play a critical role in the metabolism of energy. Consuming a diet rich in fruits, vegetables, lean meats, and whole grains can ensure you are getting these essential micronutrients.

4.7. The Importance of Regular Meals

To keep your body and brain fueled, consuming regular meals and healthy snacks is essential. Skipping meals can lead to feeling sluggish, while overeating can result in energy crashes. Aim for balanced meals packed with complex carbohydrates, lean proteins, healthy fats, and plenty of fruits and vegetables, and don't forget to snack healthy if hunger strikes in between!

4.8. Considerations for Dietary Restrictions

Of course, everyone's dietary needs are unique, and general advice may need to tailored for people with dietary restrictions or allergies. Whether you're vegetarian/vegan, gluten-intolerant, lactose intolerant, or have any other dietary restrictions, ensure your nutritional needs are met by seeking suitable alternatives or supplements.

4.9. Final Thoughts

Remember, fueling your body with the right nutrients is not about rigid meal plans or eliminating entire food groups; it's about balance, consistency, and listening to your body's needs. Your body is a complex machine, and the food you use as fuel greatly impacts its performance. Embrace the power of nutrition to supercharge your productivity and set the stage for a successful day, every day.

Ultimately, the role of nutrition extends far beyond maintaining physical well-being and powers every aspect of mental function, directly impacting our ability to function at our productive best. By arming yourself with these nutritional strategies, you arm yourself with the fuel needed to conquer each productive day with unwavering focus, unparalleled energy, and unshakeable determination.

Chapter 5. Embracing Mindfulness: The Key to Elevated Consciousness

Mindfulness, as a practice and a philosophy, stretches beyond the realm of fleeting trends and momentary fads. It's an ancient ideology finding renewed significance in our chaotic, always-connected world. Mindfulness is the key that gently uncovers the path to elevated consciousness. By nurturing a profound and deliberate connection to the present, mindfulness opens the door to a profound symbiosis of body, mind, and spirit—a twofold space of tranquility and empowerment.

5.1. Embracing Mindfulness: Understanding the Concept

The road to understanding begins with a simple question. What is mindfulness? Mindfulness, quite simply, understanding and acknowledging the present in all its complexity and beauty, without judgment or bias. It represents the cultivation of a deliberate awareness not just of our surroundings or our actions, but our thoughts and emotions as well—every sensation that constitutes the living experience.

5.2. The Benefits of Mindfulness: Unpacking the Science

Research and science walk hand-in-hand with mindfulness, providing empirical evidence that reinforces the benefits of this age-old practice. Neurological studies have shown a positive correlation between mindfulness and the development of the prefrontal cortex, an area of the brain crucial for decision-making, emotional regulation, and self-awareness. Regular practice of mindfulness exercises can reshape our brains for the better, establish greater resilience in the face of stressors, and set the stage for greater emotional well-being.

5.3. Basic Mindfulness Techniques: Starting Your Journey

To begin your journey, you'll need the tools of the trade—mindfulness techniques that you can incorporate into your daily routine.

1. **Body scanning**: A form of focused mind-body interaction, this technique involves mentally scanning your body from head to toe, observing any sensations that arise—tightness, heat, tingling, or pure neutrality. This practice fosters a heightened awareness of the bodily experience, grounding you in the present.

2. **Breath awareness**: The core of many mindfulness practices, this technique involves focusing on your breath. Feel the inhale and exhale, noting the movement of your body with each breath cycle. By attaching your conscious thoughts to your breath, you can gain a sense of anchored presence.

3. **Observation technique**: Choose an object—a plant, a piece of fruit, an everyday item. Spend a few minutes observing it, noting its shape, colour, texture, smell, if applicable. This practice cultivates a keen eye for detail, prompting you to engage more fully with the world around you.

5.4. Integrating Mindfulness in Day-to-Day Life

It may sound intimidating to add another task to your schedule, but mindfulness is not about cramming additional obligations into your already busy day. It's about integrating the practice into your existing routines—a concept known as mindful living. It could mean spending the first five minutes after waking practicing breath awareness. Or eating your meals mindfully, paying full attention to your senses as you consume your food. Even mundane tasks like washing dishes or taking a shower can be opportunities to practice mindfulness by fully immersing your senses in the experience.

5.5. Overcoming Challenges in Mindfulness Practice

Mindfulness, though profound in its simplicity, comes with its own set of hurdles. Distractions may seem overwhelming, and progress may start to seem slow or non-existent. This is where patience and persistence come in. Understand that the mindful journey is not linear but circular. Each return to the breath or body, every refocusing of the wayward mind, serves as a testament to your commitment to the path.

5.6. Tools and Apps to Assist in Mindfulness Practice

In this era of technology, numerous tools and applications can serve as aids to mindful living. Such as:

1. **Headspace**: Provides guided mindfulness meditation sessions.
2. **Calm**: Offers guided meditations, sleep stories, and mindfulness

exercises.

3. **Insight Timer**: Comes with an extensive library of free mindfulness and meditation resources.

5.7. Final Thoughts on Embracing Mindfulness

The journey to mindfulness is a pilgrimage—one marked by self-discovery, acceptance, and elevated consciousness. Embrace this voyage as a profound return to self, a journey of becoming attuned to the wonders of the present. Learn from the journey to be here now, for in the dance of life, every step is a marvel worth experiencing fully, a marvel best viewed through the lens of mindfulness.

Embarking on this profound journey opens a world of possibilities. Mindfulness provides the foundation for elevated consciousness, marking the path to a better understanding of self, deeper relationships, and ultimately, success in all walks of life. Grasp the key, unlock the door to mindfulness and open yourself to an elevated consciousness—everyday, in every way.

Chapter 6. Harnessing Time: Effective Time Management Tactics

Time management is an indispensable tool that can unlock potential, improve productivity, and reduce stress levels. It's like the compass that directs all our actions, where each tick of the clock can either chip away at the mountain of success, or build it even higher. Imagine having that unyielding command over every minute of your day, and the sheer power to convert that into a string of achievements. If such mastery over time piques your interest, then you have arrived at the right page. Let's take a grand dive into the universe of effective time management tactics, where every second counts towards building sprawling success stories.

6.1. The Foundation: Understanding Where Your Time Goes

The first step to harnessing time effectively is to understand where it is being spent. Without the knowledge of your current situation, predicting and planning for the future becomes a formidable task. Therefore, we need an analytical yet very achievable process: a Time Log.

To create a Time Log, start by tracking all your activities for a week. Note down the start and end time, and the duration for each task, be it professional or personal. Don't overlook even trivial actions — every minute counts.

Once you obtain substantial data, analyse and categorize the tasks into three broad categories:

- Productive: Tasks that contribute directly to your goals.

- Necessary: Tasks that don't contribute to your goals but must be done.

- Wasteful: Tasks that are neither productive nor necessary.

Understanding these categories and your patterns therein will give you a clearer picture of your time usage, and offer the first stepping stone towards effective time management.

6.2. Techniques for Better Time Management

Armed with the knowledge of your time use, let's explore some well-renowned techniques that can help improve time management.

6.2.1. The Eisenhower Matrix

Named after the 34th President of the United States, Dwight D. Eisenhower, this technique categorizes tasks into four quadrants based on their urgency and importance. The matrix looks like this:

```
|                        | Important | Not Important |
|------------------------|-----------|---------------|
| Urgent                 | Quadrant I | Quadrant II  |
| Not Urgent             | Quadrant III | Quadrant IV |
```

- Quadrant I consists of tasks that are both urgent and important. Tackle these first.

- Quadrant II contains tasks that are not urgent but important. These need to be planned for.

- Quadrant III holds tasks that are urgent but not important. These can be delegated.

- Quadrant IV is for tasks that are neither urgent nor important. These should be minimized or eliminated.

Using the Eisenhower Matrix, you can identify and prioritize your tasks effectively.

6.2.2. The Pomodoro Technique

The Pomodoro Technique, developed by Francesco Cirillo, has gained worldwide popularity due to its simplicity and effectiveness. Here's how it works:

- Choose a task to work on.

- Set a timer for 25 minutes (this is one Pomodoro).

- Work on the task until the timer rings. If you get distracted, reset the timer.

- Take a 5-minute break once a Pomodoro is completed.

- Repeat the process. After four Pomodoros, take a longer break of 15-30 minutes.

This approach helps maintain your focus and prevents burnout by providing scheduled breaks.

6.3. Leveraging the Power of Technology

In this digital era, we have an infinite array of tools and applications at our disposal that can assist in time management. These include project and task management tools like Trello or ClickUp, time tracking tools such as RescueTime or Clockify, and distraction blockers like StayFocusd or Freedom. Each can be customized to fit seamlessly into your routine and offer powerful insights, reminders, and automation.

Integrating these into your workflow can surely amp up your productivity and draw you closer to the profitable mastery of time.

6.4. Building a Time-Sensitive Culture

Time management isn't just about individual diligence. In a team-focused environment like an office, inculcating a time-sensitive culture is crucial. Foster respect for individual's time, encourage regular breaks, acknowledge good time management practices, and lead by example. This creates a productive ecosystem where everyone is invested in managing their time better.

Harnessing time, although a formidable skill, can bring about colossal changes in the way we approach our goals. Equipped with these potent tactics, you have the power to take control of your routine and burgeon into a success story that stands the test of time.

Chapter 7. Building Resilience: Strategies for Bouncing Back

Resilience is a term that often surfaces in discourses on personal growth, leadership, and success, and for good reason. Resilience is the capacity to grapple with adversities, setbacks, and failures, to learn from them, and to use them as stepping stones towards success. This chapter delves into the complexities of resilience, its underpinnings, the essential role it plays in the pursuit of success, and practical strategies you can use to cultivate this powerful personal quality.

7.1. Understanding Resilience and Its Importance

Resilience is likened to mental, emotional, and spiritual elasticity, the adaptive strength that enables individuals to withstand life's pressures, recover from traumas, and maintain their balance during periods of turbulence. Resilient individuals embrace failures as potent learning experiences and view setbacks not as final, but as delay, not denial.

Success, by its nature, is not a smooth ascent but a rocky road peppered with obstructions that test our mettle and commitment. Being resilient allows you to withstand these challenges, keep your focus on your goals, and realize your aspirations in spite of adversity. Moreover, resilience equips you to manage stress, regulate emotions, and establish a positive morale which is indispensable for sustaining high performance and achieving long-term success.

7.2. Developing a Resilient Mindset

Resilience is not an innate trait that we either have or don't have; it's a nurtured ability which can be strengthened with consistent effort. Let's examine how to foster a resilient mindset.

Startegy 1: Embrace a Growth Mindset

A growth mindset, introduced by psychologist Carol Dweck, involves seeing challenges as opportunities for self-improvement. Embrace the belief that abilities and intelligence can be developed through hard work, effort, and persistence. Seeing adversity as a challenge to be overcome trains your mind to be resilient.

Strategy 2: Cultivate Optimism

Maintaining a positive outlook, regardless of the situation, augments your resilience. Optimistic people confront hardships with a conviction that they will eventually surmount them. Research indicates that optimism fosters resilience by buffering against stress and facilitating adaptive coping mechanisms.

Strategy 3: Practice Self-Affirmation

Equip yourself with a cache of empowering personal affirmations. Positive self-statements boost self-esteem, foster self-efficacy, and promote resilience. You might say to yourself, "I've faced tough times before and come out stronger. I can do it again."

7.3. Reinforcing Resilience Through Habits and Practices

Let's delve into some daily practices that reinforce resilience and build your capacity to bounce back from adversity.

Practice 1: Exercise Regularly

Regular exercise does wonders for your resilience. It releases endorphins, the feel-good chemicals that boost your mood, reduce stress, and enhance your sense of wellbeing. Moreover, overcoming the daily physical challenges exercise imposes naturally builds and reinforces resilience.

Practice 2: Nurture Emotional Agility

Developing emotional agility is key to bolstering resilience. Emotional agility entails accessing and harnessing your emotions, enabling them to serve your best interests. Regularly practicing mindfulness meditation helps increase emotional agility.

Practice 3: Foster a Strong Support Network

Social support is a significant resilience booster. Nurturing a network of reliable, positive-minded friends, family, and mentors provides a buffer against life's adversities, adds to your sense of belonging, and strengthens your confidence in overcoming challenges.

Practice 4: Embrace Lifelong Learning

Commit to lifelong learning. Regularly seek knowledge and experiences that expand your perspectives, hone your skills, and nurture personal growth. Learning incites a sense of capability and resilience.

7.4. Implementing Resilience in the Face of Setbacks

When setbacks occur, and they will, it's important that your resilience kicks in immediately. Here are some steps to follow to ensure that you do not succumb to adversity.

Step 1: Accept the Situation

Acceptance is the starting point of resilience. Acknowledge the situation instead of denying or avoiding it. Recognize the reality of what has happened.

Step 2: Practice Mindful Reflection

Reflect on your situation mindfully without being overly critical. What can you learn from what happened? Seeing setbacks as an opportunity for introspection and learning triggers your resilience.

Step 3: Formulate a Plan of Action

Once you've absorbed the situation and derived some lessons from it, it's time to plan your comeback. A proactive approach makes you feel more control over your circumstances, enhancing resilience.

Step 4: Implement the Plan

The final and most important step is to carry out your plan. Action is the antidote to despair. Even if you start small, consistent forward steps will signal your resilient response and reignite your drive towards your goals.

As we conclude, remember that developing resilience is a lifelong journey. It's built through countless moments of courage, perseverance, and learning from failures. It's fostered in day-to-day perseverance, the efforts we dodge life's punches, get back on our feet after a fall, and push forward with determination and hope. As you leverage these strategies and practices, remember to be patient with yourself. One step at a time, you're becoming a stronger, more resilient version of yourself, equipped to conquer any challenge in pursuit of your dreams. Harnessing resilience is indeed, building an unshakeable foundation for success.

Chapter 8. Boosting Productivity: Tools and Techniques

To truly master any endeavor in life, productivity is quintessential. In this chapter, we bring to the table multifaceted tools and techniques focused on significantly enhancing productivity, thereby accelerating you on your path to success.

8.1. Harnessing Technology to Boost Productivity

Arguably, one of the most prevalent and potent tools to significantly improve productivity is technology. Software and hardware products designed specifically to improve efficiency and productivity are plentiful in today's technological landscape.

One core tool includes project management platforms such as Trello, Asana, or Basecamp. These platforms present a unified workspace where one can organize, delegate, and track the progression of different tasks within a larger project. They essentially serve as your navigator through the sea of work you need to handle, keeping everything neatly organized and accessible.

Another set of tools that warrant mentioning are communication platforms, like Slack or Microsoft Teams. Modern work, whether personal or professional, often requires collaboration. Through such platforms, real-time conversations can facilitate quicker decision-making and problem-solving processes, while eliminating the hassle of back-and-forth emails.

Moreover, time-tracking tools such as Toggl or TimeCamp, can be instrumental in providing insights into how you are spending your time and help identify areas where it can be better invested.

Finally, apps like RescueTime can keep your digital distractions in check, thus freeing time for tasks that truly matter. Leverage technology to work smarter, not harder.

8.2. Techniques to Improve Focus and Eliminate Distractions

Focus is the distinguishing feature between aimless effort and meaningful productivity. Several techniques have been proven to improve focus and eliminate distractions.

One such technique is the Pomodoro Technique. The principle is to work for 25 minutes (one Pomodoro) and then take a five-minute break. Every fourth break should be a longer 15-minutes. This approach can help maintain concentration over extended periods while also preventing burnout.

Another technique involves creating an environment conducive to productivity. Clear your workspace of distractions, employ ambient sound or music if it aids your concentration, and ensure the area is well-lit to reduce strain on your eyes.

Additionally, making use of the Eisenhower box, a matrix that helps categorize tasks based on their urgency and importance, can make a world of difference in how you perceive and tackle your tasks.

8.3. Mindset and Behavior: Keys to Boosted Productivity

Cultivating a productivity-enhancing mindset and behavior is as crucial as having the right tools and techniques at your disposal. A growth mindset, characterized by the belief in one's ability to learn and improve, can prove transformative.

Inculcating habits such as daily goal setting, regular breaks, exercise, and mindfulness practice can profoundly improve mental clarity and focus. Regular rewards for task completion can also serve as a strong motivational factor.

Constructive behaviors also involve understanding when to say no. Over-commitment can dilute efforts and stall progress. Learning to prioritize your tasks effectively is crucial.

You are in the driver's seat, and your mind is the engine. Nurture the right mindset, and you'll be amazed by the heights you can reach.

8.4. Consistency: The Underlying Principle of Productivity

Last but certainly not least, it's critical to understand the importance of consistency. The most robust tool or effective technique would bring futile results without the consistency of effort.

Aim to establish a routine that incorporates these tools and techniques, and stick to it. Over time, you'll develop increased resilience towards distractions and improved overall productivity.

In conclusion, productivity is an ongoing journey of growth and refinement. The tools and techniques discussed can act as catalysts on this journey, providing the momentum you need. Start incorporating these into your daily routine and watch productivity skyrocket, allowing your dreams to translate into reality. After all, productivity isn't about being busy; it's about being effective. master the art of productivity and you'll unlock a world of potential you never thought possible.

Chapter 9. Cultivating Relationships: Networking for Success

The concept of networking is far from a modern invention. It has been the underpinning strategy of successful people throughout history. In the context of 'Daily Mastery', networking does not merely mean professional networking for career advancement; it equally applies to developing personal relationships that are supportive, inspiring, and inherently rewarding. When observed strategically, networking becomes an essential pillar of success. Let's dive deep into the many elements of networking that will empower and gear you for success.

9.1. The Fundamentals of 'Networking'

Networking essentially revolves around creating and nurturing relationships. It includes connecting with others, understanding their perspectives, assertively communicating your ideas, maintaining meaningful associations, contributing positively to conversations, recognizing opportunities, and above all, sharing a part of yourself to those around you.

Networking also involves recognising the value of connections, not just with high-status individuals, but with anyone who has an interesting story to tell, or a valuable lesson to share. Every individual you meet has something unique to offer. Possessing the insight to recognize these opportunities and the willingness to learn from them is a key part of successful networking.

9.2. Strategic Networking for Success

Strategic networking is all about being intentional. It is about understanding your goals and pursuing connections in a way that helps you to achieve them. Benefit-fueled rapport with leaders, think-tanks, fellow enthusiasts, potential mentors, or influencers in your relevant arena can lead to incredible breakthroughs.

1. Identify Your Goals: Understand what you hope to achieve from networking. Is it knowledge, opportunities, direction, mentorship, or partnerships? Once your goals are clear, your network can be more targeted.

2. Choose the Right Platform: Select suitable platforms, both online and offline, where you are most likely to meet individuals who align with your purpose and vision.

3. Approach Authentically: Always be your genuine self while networking. Authenticity leads to trust, which is vital for any successful relationship.

4. Offer Value: Networking is not just about receiving; it's equally about giving. Before you can expect to take something away from a conversation, think about what you can contribute.

Remember, strategic networking is not transactional; it's about building genuine relationships.

9.3. The Power of Active Listening in Networking

Active listening, an underrated skill, is an esteemed attribute of successful networkers. It involves attentively listening to others, processing their information and responding thoughtfully. It can foster deeper relationships, build trust, and generate meaningful dialogues. Give the speaker your undivided attention, be open-minded, ask insightful questions, and demonstrate understanding through related responses. Offer feedback positively, and acknowledge the thought-process of others. Respect in conversation attracts lasting relationships.

9.4. The Impact of Digital Networking

In the current digital age, online networking has opened doors to global connections. Social networking platforms, professional forums, online communities, webinars, and virtual events provide invaluable opportunities. Using these platforms effectively can result in exponential personal and professional growth.

Engage frequently and constructively on these platforms, share your views and invite others to do the same. Leverage the power of digital networking to expand your horizons, develop a diverse network of contacts, and gain global perspectives.

9.5. Maintaining Long-Term Relationships

The work of networking doesn't end at making connections; maintaining them is equally, if not more, important. Regular communication is crucial, but it should never feel forced. Keep up with significant milestones, express gratitude for their help and support, and be there during their adversity. Implement patience, flexibility, and authenticity in your interactions, and in the way you value your relationships.

In conclusion, networking is an integral part of success. It is a continuous journey of building, sustaining, revitalizing, and cherishing connections that add mutual value. Developing relationships through strategic networking can bless you with a wealth of wisdom, nurture personal and professional growth, boost your confidence, provide you with broader viewpoints, and guide you towards the path of success. Remember, the essence of networking lies in reciprocation. So, approach it with a motivational spirit that is both prepared to learn from others and eager to contribute to their lives as well.

Chapter 10. Developing Leadership: Creating Influence and Impact

Leadership is a multifaceted discipline that is essential for anyone who wants to excel in their personal or professional life. It comprises not just management, but also the ability to inspire, influence, and make a significant impact. Whether you are an entrepreneur seeking to take your business to new heights, a professional trying to level up the corporate ladder, or someone seeking to make a difference in your community, cultivating strong leadership capabilities is integral in your journey towards mastery.

10.1. The Essence of Leadership

The essence of leadership is rooted in the ability to influence others towards a shared goal. However, influence isn't derived from control or manipulation. Instead, it comes from a place of understanding, respect, and genuine care for those you're leading.

While the concept of influence might seem abstract, science has been able to break it down into comprehendible aspects. One way to understand and develop influence is through the "Influence Model" developed by psychologists Robert Cialdini and Noah Goldstein. This model includes six principles: Reciprocity, Consistency, Social proof, Authority, Liking, and Scarcity. Leveraging these principles while walking your leadership path can help you create a substantial impact on those around you.

The second critical element of leadership hinges on creating impact. Impact is more than the sum of your individual actions; it is the ripple effect that those actions create. It's how your influence changes practices, attitudes, and even lives.

10.2. Cultivating Influence: A Strategic Approach

Cultivating influence requires a strategic approach. Begin by establishing strong connections with those around you. Foster an environment of trust and empathy, by demonstrating your own authenticity and honesty. When people believe you're genuine and have their best interests at heart, they're more willing to be influenced by you.

Consider the Reciprocity principle — if you provide value first, others are more likely to return the favor. This can be as simple as sharing knowledge, offering support in difficult situations, or even just lending an open ear when needed.

Next, build consistent and reliable behaviors, aligning yourself with the Consistency principle. Your words and actions must be congruent, as this builds a reputation for integrity. With credibility, you can influence more effectively.

Also, recognize that in the modern world, your influence doesn't stop at your immediate connections. Through the power of social media and digital platforms, you can leverage the Social Proof principle to extend your reach. By showcasing testimonials, reviews, and endorsements, others can see the positive effect of your leadership.

10.3. Creating Impact: Leadership that Transcends

To transition from merely influencing to creating a significant impact, you need to advocate change that goes beyond individual motivations and contributes to larger purposes. Think of impact in terms of measurable changes in attitudes, behaviors, and beliefs of those around you.

Start impacting others by setting clear and compelling visions that resonate with their aspirations. Be the torchbearer, illuminifying the path towards the common objectives, fueled by your shared values.

However, merely setting visions is not sufficient. Impactful leaders actively work on realizing those visions by developing actionable strategies and enabling their team with needed resources and motivation. They are not afraid to challenge the status quo, and their relentless pursuit of goals instills a sense of confidence and aspiration in their followers.

Moreover, remember that making an impact isn't a one-and-done effort. It requires continuously assessing your actions and their results, learning, and refining your methods over time. It's a journey about iterative improvement and relentless pursuit.

10.4. Moving Forward: The Continuous Growth of Leadership

In leadership, as with any other skill, complacency is the opposite of growth. Aspiring leaders relentlessly strive to improve their capabilities. They seek continuous learning experiences, challenge their assumptions, and never shy away from feedback. They understand that their growth will reflect in their ability to influence and make an impact.

As you grow in your leadership journey, keep an open mind and heart. Stay curious, ask questions, embrace diversities, and always remember that leadership is less about commanding and more about rallying others towards shared success. Remember, the goal of influential and impactful leadership is not just about achieving a goal but about creating a meaningful journey towards that goal.

In conclusion, leadership goes beyond mere management — it's about creating influence and making an impact. To develop exceptional leadership skills, adopt a growth mindset, foster strong relationships, and keep refining your approach based on feedback and learnings. Remember, becoming an influential leader with an impactful reach is a journey, not a destination. So, be patient with yourself, celebrate your small wins, and continue pushing the boundaries of what you can achieve.

Chapter 11. Sustained Momentum: Keeping the Flame Alive

Continuing on a successful trajectory is a task that requires unyielding persistence, relight enthusiasm, and an unflinching will to succeed. Following the breakthroughs in productivity, the victory over time, and the mastery of resilience, the final hurdle remains of sustaining the momentum you've managed to build. How do you keep the flame alight? How can you assure that a momentary blaze of inspiration doesn't fizzle out into ashes?

11.1. The Perpetual Machine: Understanding Momentum

Momentum, from the Latin word 'movimentum', signifies movement and motion. For our context, we define it as a continuous unstoppable force that propels an individual towards their objectives, akin to a snowball rolling down a hill, growing larger and faster with each passing second. When we speak about your momentum in the realm of personal or professional growth, we refer to the ongoing progress, the habitual forward thrust that draws you closer to your dreams each day.

However, momentum isn't a self-sustaining phenomenon. It requires continual nurturing and conscious effort. It is a delicate yet powerful tool, easy to lose yet difficult to stop when truly harnessed. Imagine your momentum as a bonfire. Initially, the flames are small and require constant attention; you need to add more wood, control the wind and ensure the flame doesn't die out. But once the flames grow larger, they're self-sustaining, needing less immediate care but more strategic maintenance, preventing it from becoming an unruly forest fire.

11.2. The Fire Keepers: Constant Fuel for Your Internal Flame

So, how do you keep your inner fire alive and prevent the flame from turning into dust? The answer is three-fold: setting long-term objectives, celebrating small victories, and embracing a growth mindset.

Long-term objectives act as the North Star, providing you with a direction to navigate through life's tricky terrains. They serve as the vision for the future you desire, guiding your daily actions. When setting these objectives, aim for specificity. Ambiguity only breeds confusion; the more defined your goals are, the clearer your path will be.

The second element, celebrating small victories, helps you recognize and appreciate the steps forward, however minor they may seem. Every triumphant moment, every task crossed off your list, is a brick towards the massive edifice of your dreams. Recognizing these achievements gives you a sense of progress, a validation of your efforts, fostering motivation and boosting esteem.

Finally, nurturing a growth mindset, that frames obstacles as opportunities and failures as lessons, fosters resilience, encouraging you to persevere even in the face of adversities. Treating setbacks merely as challenges to overcome feeds the flame of your internal drive, providing a consistent source of fuel for your momentum.

11.3. Keep Rolling: Cultivating Daily Habits that Propel Progress

Just as a rolling stone gathers no moss, a person in constant advancement gathers no stagnation. The cornerstone of sustained momentum is a strong foundation in daily consistent habits. Here are some strategies to incorporate into your routine:

1. **Plan Ahead**: Prior planning not only aids in executing tasks efficiently but also offers a clear outlook of the tasks, helping avoid the anxiety and stress of unplanned surprises.

2. **Prioritize**: Use tools such as the Eisenhower Matrix to distinguish between the urgent and necessary, helping you focus on what's truly important.

3. **Practice Self-care**: Prioritize physical and mental health, ensuring you're in optimal shape to tackle tasks.

4. **Seek Feedback and Learn**: Constant learning and open-mindedness prevents stagnation and fuels continuous improvement.

5. **Stay Motivated**: Motivation is the wind to the sails of your momentum, maintain it through visualization techniques and affirmations.

Remember, succeeding doesn't just involve riding the wave of inspiration and motivation, it involves paddling out to meet that wave and riding it all the way to the shore. The art of sustaining momentum is a dance, a delicate interplay of forces kept in equilibrium by steadfast resolve, unyielding resilience, and an indefatigable spirit. By celebrating small victories, nurturing a growth mindset, setting long-term clear objectives, and instilling potent daily habits, you can keep your flame alive and let its light guide you to your coveted goals. Thus concludes our exploration of sustaining momentum, and with that, a step further into mastery of our daily journey towards success.